John Miller's

Trumpet

Basics

A method for individual and group learning

B♭ trumpet or cornet

With illustrations by Drew Hillier

for June Wilkinson and Antonia Altham

FABER *ff* MUSIC

Contents

3 A message to you

4 The instrument

4 Before you begin …

6 *Stage 1*

8 *Stage 2*

10 *Stage 3*

12 *Stage 4*

14 *Stage 5* 2/4 ⌢ slurs

16 *Stage 6* A *f* *p*

18 *Stage 7* F♯ F♮ ♯ ♮

20 *Stage 8* B B ties key signatures

23 *Stage 9* C ♪ *mf*

26 *Stage 10* 1st and 2nd time bars

28 *Stage 11* B♭ B♭ 5/4 ♭ *ff*

31 *Stage 12*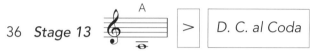

34 Concert pieces 1

36 *Stage 13*

39 *Stage 14* G♯ ♯o 𝄿 minor scales

42 *Stage 15*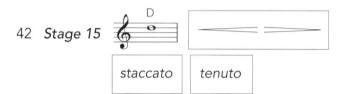

45 *Stage 16*

48 *Stage 17* E♭ 6/8

51 *Stage 18* chromatic scale

54 *Stage 19* E ♫

57 *Stage 20* blues scale improvisation

60 Concert pieces 2

63 Fingering chart

64 Acknowledgements

64 Additional resources

Unless stated otherwise, all musical content is by John Miller.

A message to you

Welcome to *Trumpet Basics* – the tutor that will guide you through the first steps in learning to play cornet or trumpet.

The trumpet can play everything from solemn fanfares to exciting jazz; the cornet, its flexible friend, is the indispensable solo instrument in every brass band. And *Trumpet Basics* will set you on the path for all these future challenges: very soon you'll be able to play real tunes, play with others, and know your way around the instrument.

To help you on your way, here are a few hot tips:

- Your teacher is important. There is no better start than copying a good player.
- Play a little each day rather than a lot the day before your lesson. This builds up your playing muscles and keeps your brain engaged.
- Look after your instrument. This book will show you how.
- If you're not sure about anything, ask your teacher to explain it or, best of all, to play it to you.
- Make music with others. This is fun and teaches you how to listen and play at the same time. There are lots of duets and group pieces in this book.
- Ask your teacher or somebody else to play the piano and trumpet accompaniments that are included in the Teacher's book; these are indicated by the following icons:
  - 🧍 for trumpet duet parts
  - ⏸ for piano accompaniments.
- Always use the backing tracks (X) when you can. If you have the CD edition, these are included; if not, they can be accessed from fabermusicstore.com/basics. If you want to change the tempo (speed) of a track, there are many programmes available on the internet that will do this for free.
- Go out of your way to hear good players (especially in live performances).
- Grab every opportunity to play in public either as a soloist or in a group; after all, this is one of the main reasons for playing an instrument.

The biggest tip of all is to enjoy your playing! That's always been my secret …

John Miller

Trumpet Basics checklist

You will need:
- A trumpet or cornet
- A good quality mouthpiece
- Mouthpiece cleaning brush, plus a flexible 'pull through'
- Valve oil and slide grease
- Music stand
- Pencil
- *Trumpet Basics*

The trumpet

The trumpet was used as a signalling instrument in Ancient China, Egypt and Scandinavia, and as a ceremonial instrument by the Romans. (You may also have heard about seven trumpets blowing down the walls of Jericho!) The instrument was initially a simple long tube with no valves – the three buttons you press down – and players played different notes by controlling their lips and the air. Around 1815 valves were invented, instantly making brass instruments more musically flexible, and they were soon added to the trumpet.

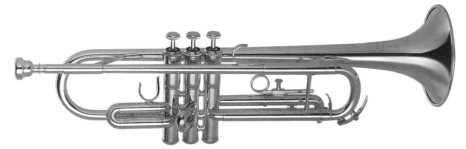

The cornet

The cornet (meaning 'little horn') first appeared in Paris around 1828, and was at first a coiled post-horn with valves. It became very popular as a solo instrument in early jazz through players like Louis Armstrong, and is a major instrument in brass bands. Today both cornets and trumpets are made of brass, either lacquered or silver-plated, and appear in brass bands, symphony orchestras, wind and brass ensembles, jazz and pop music.

Before you begin ...

Posture

Good posture makes playing easy and enjoyable!

- Keep your arms out at 45° so that the chest is free.
- Stand or sit feeling tall, but relaxed – particularly your shoulders.
- If you are standing, keep your knees flexible and your feet hip-width apart.
- If you are sitting, keep your back away from the chair back, and have your feet flat on the floor.

Holding the instrument

Left hand Your left hand should grip the instrument lightly. You shouldn't feel like you are squashing a coke can!

Right hand Keep fingers 1, 2 and 3 on the valve caps at all times, and slightly bent; the little finger is best resting on top of the finger hook. Put a wine cork in the finger hook whilst learning this book.

The 'chops' (facial and lip muscles)

- Keep the mouthpiece above and below the red of the lips. This is important!
- When playing, avoid puffing out the cheeks. The playing muscles are all round the lower face.

How to make a sound

When playing any brass instrument, it is the vibration of the lips that creates the sound.

- Without either mouthpiece or instrument, set your lips as if to say 'em' and imagine the inside of your mouth saying 'oo'. Blowing through the lips will create a small gap in the centre, and (with practice) a raspberry-like buzz. Can you hold a steady buzz?
- Now try the above through the mouthpiece only. Find an easy note and see if you can hold it for five seconds.
- Finally, put the mouthpiece in the instrument, press down the first valve with your first right-hand finger, breathe naturally, and try your first real note.

This will probably be an F (this is the second-lowest note you can play with the first valve).

When playing the trumpet, thinking of the syllable 'TOO—' can help to form a good note.

Top tip

Two minutes of mouthpiece buzzing per day is good for your playing. Hold the mouthpiece lightly with second finger and thumb. Imagine the sound of a bee – can you buzz different shapes?

There are lots of buzzing exercises throughout *Trumpet Basics* for you to try.

Stage 1

New notes F and G

F   G

1   0

Fact file

- Notes are written on a five-lined **stave**.
- The symbol at the beginning of each stave is called a **treble clef**.
- Music is divided into units of time – **bars** or **measures** – by **barlines**. A double barline shows the end of a piece.
- The ∨ symbol shows a **breath mark**. Breathe here!

Top tip

In *Trumpet Basics*, fingering is shown in square boxes:
1 first valve down
0 open (no fingers down)

Rhythm box

♩ minim/half note: 2 beats
▬ minim/half-note rest: 2 beats
o semibreve/whole note: 4 beats

Clap:
Count: 1 2 3 4   1 2 3 4   1 2 3 4

2 Up and down

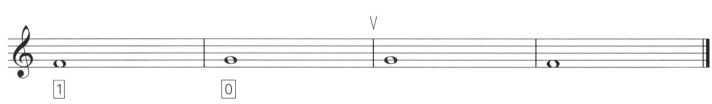

1   0

3 Wavy line

4 First things first

Top tip
Think 'TOO—TOO—TOO—'
for good note shapes.

5 Mirror image

6 The first digit

7 No stopping

8 Hippo march

5

Top tip

When you put your
instrument in the case
after playing, always put
the mouthpiece in its
special place or holder.
Otherwise it may cause
expensive dents!

Activity box

☐ Can you do this note sum? ♩ + ♩ + 𝅝 = _____

☐ What does this symbol mean: V ? _____

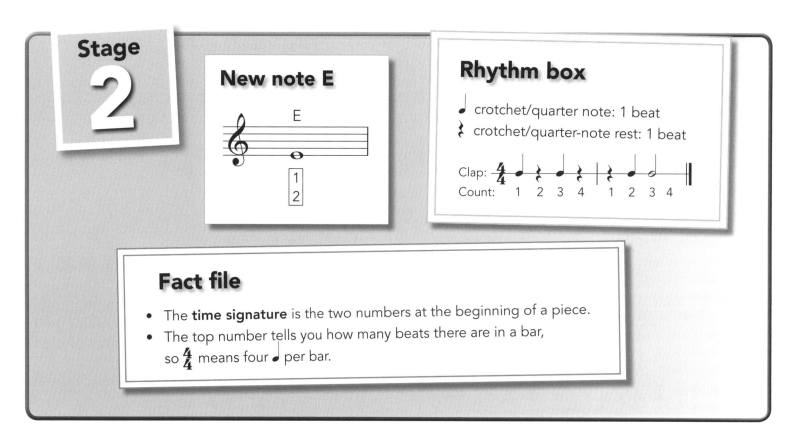

New note E

E

1
2

Rhythm box

♩ crotchet/quarter note: 1 beat
𝄽 crotchet/quarter-note rest: 1 beat

Clap:
Count: 1 2 3 4 | 1 2 3 4

Fact file

- The **time signature** is the two numbers at the beginning of a piece.
- The top number tells you how many beats there are in a bar,
  so **4/4** means four ♩ per bar.

Mouthpiece buzzing

Can you buzz this shape?

Now hold a steady pitch!

Top tip

Whether you sit or stand,
think tall and relaxed.
This makes playing easier.

9 **Happy Harry**

0   1   1
          2

10 **Watch your step!**

Watch your step!

4

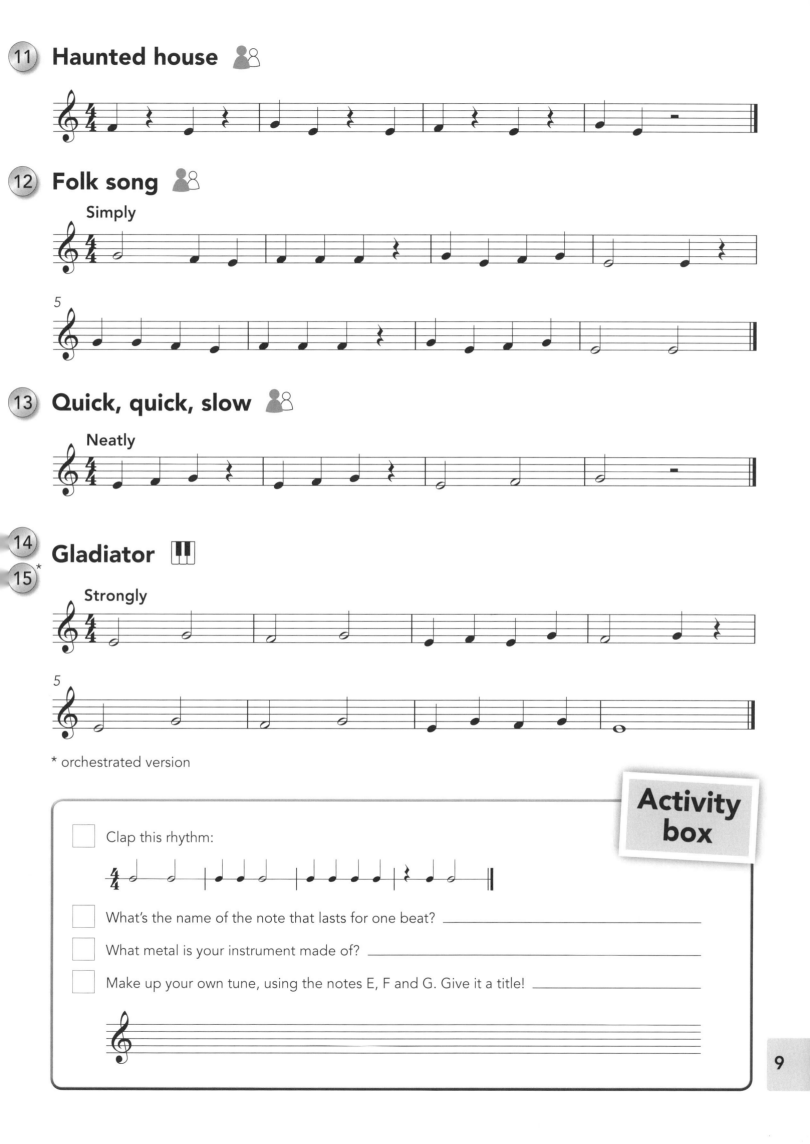

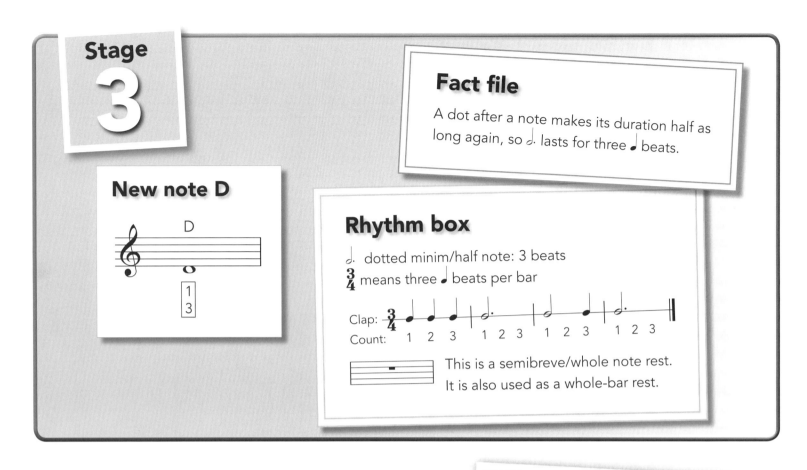

Stage 3

Fact file

A dot after a note makes its duration half as long again, so 𝅗𝅥. lasts for three 𝅘𝅥 beats.

New note D

Rhythm box

𝅗𝅥. dotted minim/half note: 3 beats

$\frac{3}{4}$ means three 𝅘𝅥 beats per bar

This is a semibreve/whole note rest.
It is also used as a whole-bar rest.

Top tip

Try this exercise played normally and buzzed on the mouthpiece.

Mouthpiece buzzing

16 Quick march

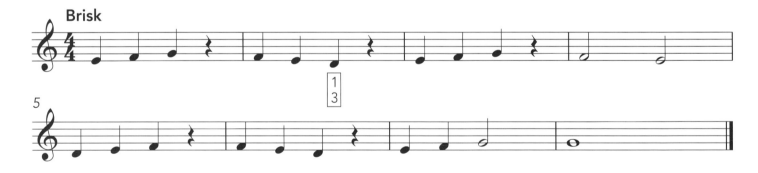

17 Sad tale

18 Any old iron?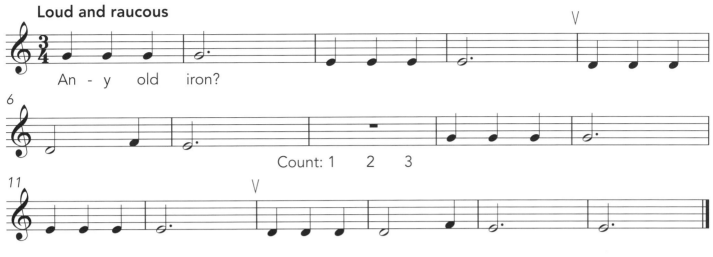

Loud and raucous

An - y old iron?

Count: 1 2 3

Try making up your own words for this piece.

19 Count as you play

In strict time

Top tip

Oil your valves often (most days), but – IMPORTANT – slide them out one at a time with care. One or two drops of oil for each valve will be plenty.

Activity box

Clap this rhythm. Can you spot which tune it comes from?

_____

What is a time signature? _____

Draw a dotted minim/half note here: _____

♩ + ♩ + 𝄽 = _____ beats.

11

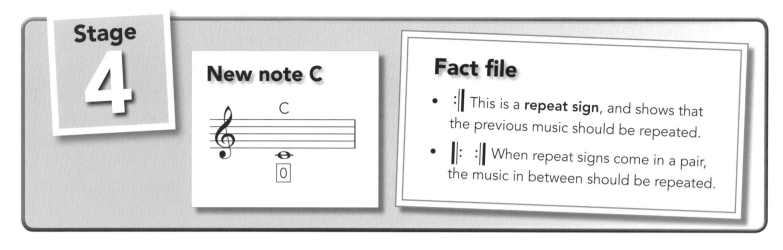

Stage 4

New note C

C

Fact file

- :|| This is a **repeat sign**, and shows that the previous music should be repeated.

- ||: :|| When repeat signs come in a pair, the music in between should be repeated.

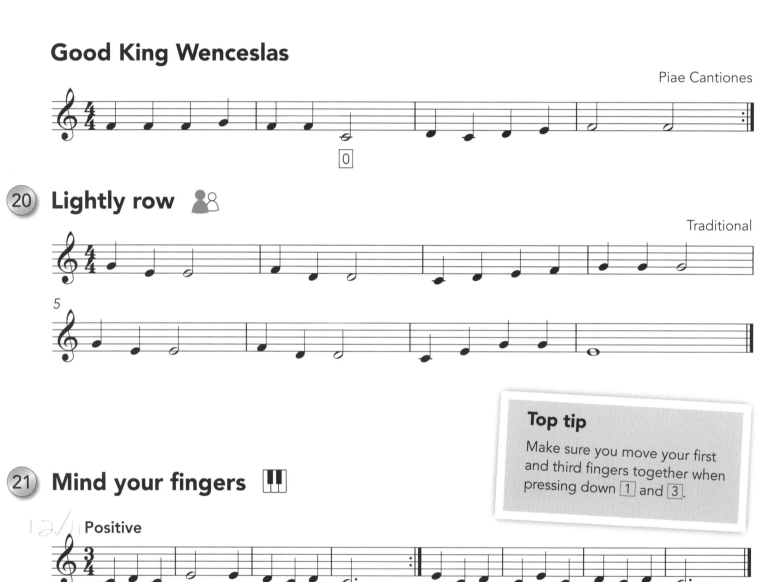

Good King Wenceslas

Piae Cantiones

20 Lightly row

Traditional

Top tip

Make sure you move your first and third fingers together when pressing down 1 and 3.

21 Mind your fingers

Positive

22 Hansel and Gretel

Engelbert Humperdinck

Singing style

Trumpet tennis (duet)

Cornet menace (duet)

☐ Which tune has the following rhythm? _____

☐ What is a treble clef? Can you draw one? (Start in the middle)

☐ What do the valves do on your instrument? _____

☐ Make up a short waltz (a dance in 3/4), using the notes C-D-E-F-G. Start and end on a C.
Give your piece a title.

_____ by _____

13

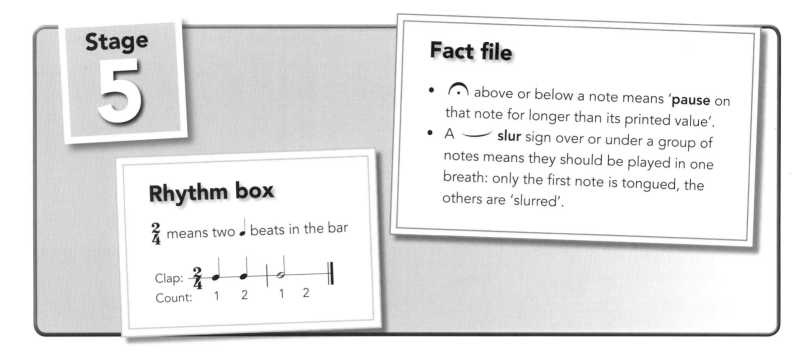

How it works

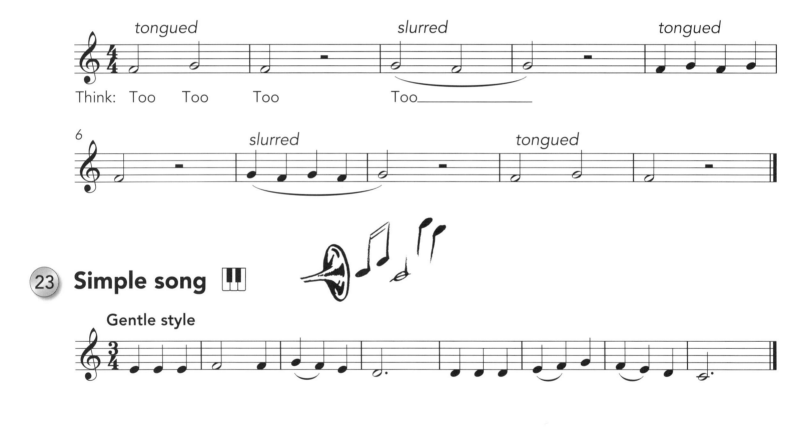

(23) **Simple song** 🎹

(24) **That does it!** 🎹

(25)*

* orchestrated version

(26) Smooth 'n' groovy

Smoothly

(27)
(28)* O when the saints

Lots of spirit!

Spiritual

* version with trumpet and piano accompaniment

Jingle bells   Can you complete this 'by ear' – with no music?

etc.

Top tip

Practise for no more than 15 minutes at a time. Enjoy a little playing each day.

Activity box

Match up these time signatures with the correct number of beats.

2/4
4/4
3/4

15

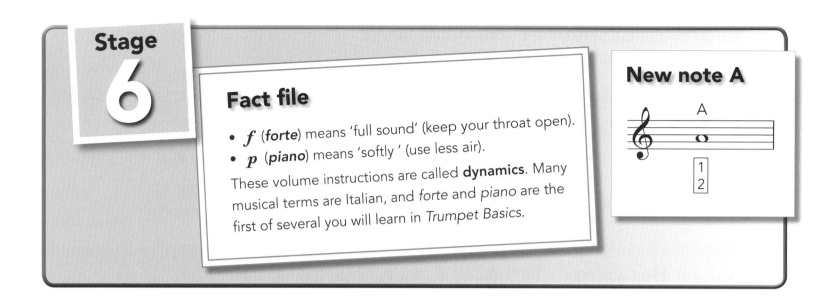

Stage 6

Fact file

- **_f_** (**forte**) means 'full sound' (keep your throat open).
- **_p_** (**piano**) means 'softly' (use less air).

These volume instructions are called **dynamics**. Many musical terms are Italian, and _forte_ and _piano_ are the first of several you will learn in _Trumpet Basics_.

New note A

The six steps

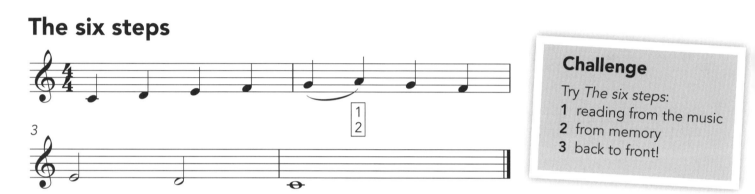

Challenge

Try _The six steps_:
1 reading from the music
2 from memory
3 back to front!

From the notes you have learnt so far, you can play _Twinkle, twinkle, little star_. Start on a C.

Warm up those chops

Freely – make your best sound

Now buzz this piece on the mouthpiece.

29 The green man

from Playford's _Dancing Master_

Singing style

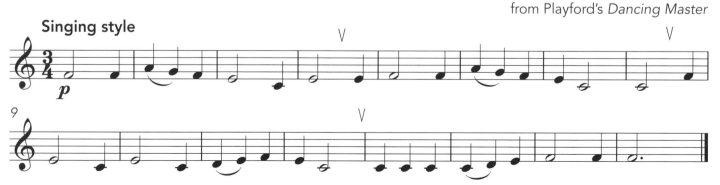

Old Macdonald's echo

Traditional English

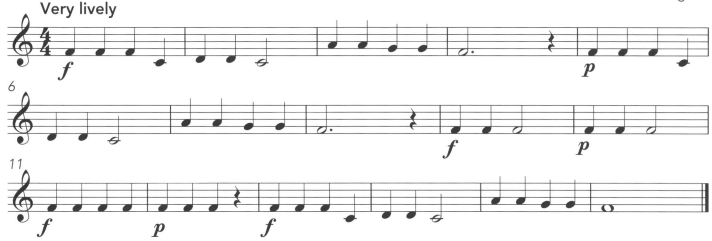

Traffic jam

In this piece, choose your own notes. A thin line means play softly;
a thick line means strongly (think of a 'thick' column of air)!

The galley slaves (duet)

* (He was famous for playing ◡ ...

Stage 7

New notes F♯ and F♮

Fact file

- Not all music starts on the first beat of the bar. Notes that come before the first full bar are called **upbeats**; the value of the upbeat is taken away from the last bar of the piece.
- A **sharp sign** (♯) in front of a note raises it by a semitone (half a tone, half step). F up to G is a whole tone; F up to F♯ is a semitone. Listen to the difference. A sharp sign (♯) is cancelled by a **natural sign** (♮).
- Sharps (♯) and naturals (♮) – and flats (♭), which you will learn about in Stage 11 – are called **accidentals**.

Important rule
Accidentals maintain their effect until the end of a bar.

Half a mo' (duet)

(31) Ode to Joy

Ludwig van Beethoven

18

32 **Lottery loser** 🎹

The Camptown races (duet)

Stephen Foster

> ### Top tip
>
> Once every month:
> - Wash your instrument in warm (not hot) soapy water.
> - Grease the valve slides.
> - Clean the inside of your mouthpiece with a special small brush.

Activity box

- [ ] What does a sharp (♯) do? _____
- [ ] What does a natural (♮) do? _____
- [ ] Choose a favourite piece from earlier in the book and try to learn it from memory.

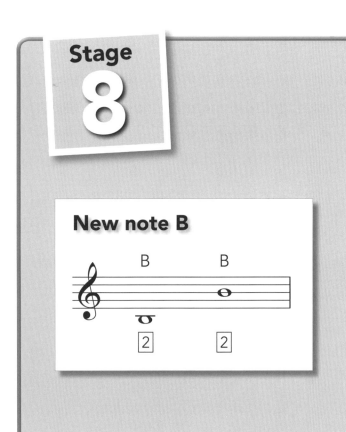

Stage 8

New note B

Fact file

- Most pieces of music are in a **key**. The **key signature** is the group of sharps or flats shown at the beginning of every stave after the clef – it tells you what key the piece is in.
- **G major** has a key signature of one sharp, as in *No, no, no, no, Geordie Munroe*. All Fs become F♯ unless cancelled by a ♮.
- A curved line joining two notes of the same pitch is called a **tie**. The length of tied notes is their combined value, so ♩‿♩ = hold for three beats.
- Just as words are grouped into sentences, notes are grouped into musical **phrases**. These are sometimes shown by a long curved line over or under the notes, called a **phrase mark**.

33
34*
Smooth as silk

Smooth and even phrases

* orchestrated version

35
Kum ba yah

Traditional African

Broadly

6

11

36 The old temple

Steady and solemn

Traditional Chinese

37 No, no, no, no, Geordie Munroe

David Haggart

Jauntily

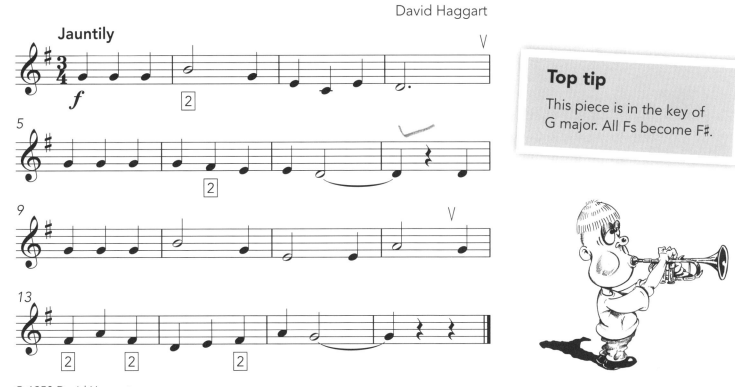

Top tip

This piece is in the key of G major. All Fs become F#.

© 1958 David Haggart

This next piece features phrase marks. Repeated notes can be gently tongued.

38 A vision for you

Brother Martin's round (for up to four players)

A round is a piece in which several players have the same music but start one after the other.
In this piece, start four bars apart.

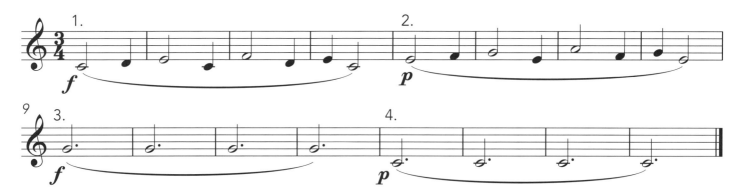

Top tip

Controlling long phrases is a valuable skill. Practise this by gently blowing against a strip of paper: tear a 3cm-wide strip of newspaper about 30cm long, hold it 15cm away from your nose and see how long you can hold the paper steady at 45°.

Word search

Find the following words in this word search:

Trumpet

Allegretto

Minim

Crotchet

Mouthpiece

Bar

Slur

Legato

Crescendo

Flat

Sharp

Rhythm

Brass

A	C	R	O	T	C	H	E	T	M
R	L	M	I	N	I	M	I	O	B
H	A	L	H	L	E	R	U	N	R
Y	P	B	E	T	E	T	U	I	A
T	N	R	B	G	H	G	O	L	S
H	R	O	A	P	R	F	A	P	S
M	I	I	I	H	D	E	L	T	R
O	C	E	T	O	S	I	T	A	O
R	C	T	R	U	M	P	E	T	T
E	C	R	E	S	C	E	N	D	O

Stage 9

New note C

C

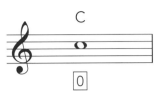

0

Rhythm box

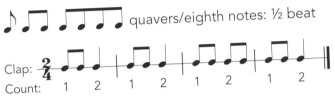
quavers/eighth notes: ½ beat

Clap: **2/4**
Count: 1 2 | 1 2 | 1 2 | 1 2

2 means 2 bars' rest

For two bars' rest in **2/4** time, count: **1** 2 | **2** 2
For two bars' rest in **3/4** time, count: **1** 2 3 | **2** 2 3

Fact file

- A **scale** is a set of notes going up or down by step. The scale of **C major** includes all the notes in the key of C major – there are no sharps or flats in this key signature.
- An **arpeggio** is made up of the first, third and fifth notes of the scale. You now know the notes of the **octave** (eight notes), from C to C.
- *mf* (**mezzo-forte**) means 'quite strong'.
- *Moderato* means 'at a moderate speed'.

C major scale

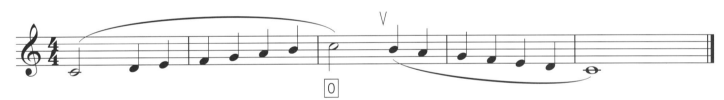

C major arpeggio

Challenge

Try the scale:
1 slurred as shown
2 all tongued
3 from memory!
4 buzzed on the mouthpiece.

23

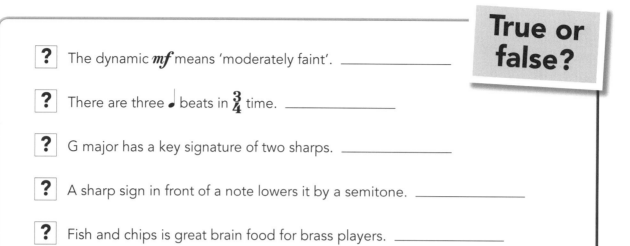

? The dynamic *mf* means 'moderately faint'. _____

? There are three ♩ beats in **3/4** time. _____

? G major has a key signature of two sharps. _____

? A sharp sign in front of a note lowers it by a semitone. _____

? Fish and chips is great brain food for brass players. _____

39 Fish 'n' chips variation

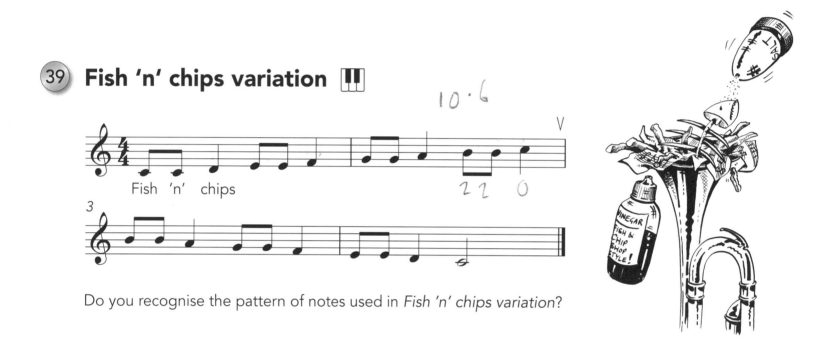

Fish 'n' chips

Do you recognise the pattern of notes used in *Fish 'n' chips variation*?

40 Postman Pat

Brian Daley

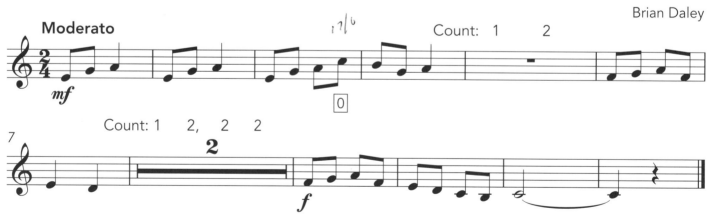

Moderato

Count: 1 2

Count: 1 2, 2 2

41 Carnival of Venice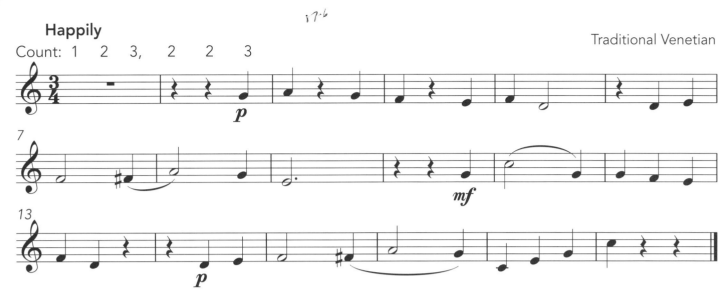

Happily

Count: 1 2 3, 2 2 3

Traditional Venetian

p

7

mf

13

p

p

42 Listening power (trio)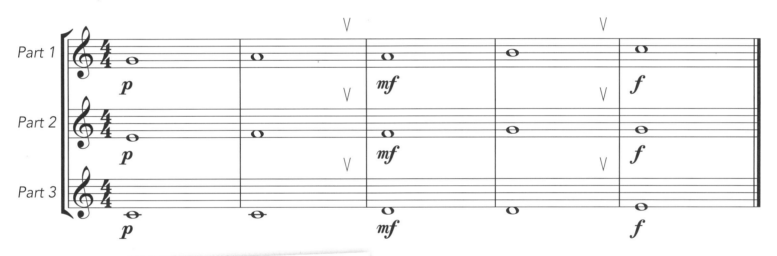

Make your best sound, listen to your neighbour, 'tune in'.

Part 1

p *mf* *f*

Part 2

p *mf* *f*

Part 3

p *mf* *f*

Top tip

Try to practise at the same time and in the same place, each day. Keep a practice diary.

Activity box

Develop your musical skills by playing familiar music by ear.
This is something jazz players are really good at. Try these:

1 *God Save the Queen* (start on a G)

2 *Eastenders Theme* (start on a C)

To help you get started, write down the first bar of each tune here:

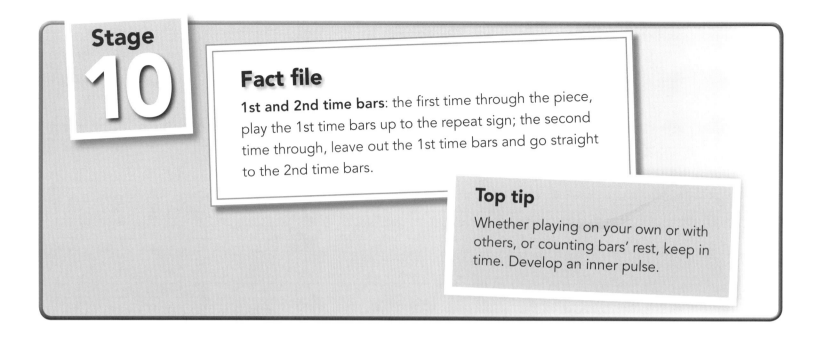

Fact file

1st and **2nd time bars**: the first time through the piece, play the 1st time bars up to the repeat sign; the second time through, leave out the 1st time bars and go straight to the 2nd time bars.

Top tip

Whether playing on your own or with others, or counting bars' rest, keep in time. Develop an inner pulse.

Slurring down

Blow right through the top notes – and don't arrive at the bottom with a bump!

43 Woozy cat waltz

44 Kalinka

Traditional Russian

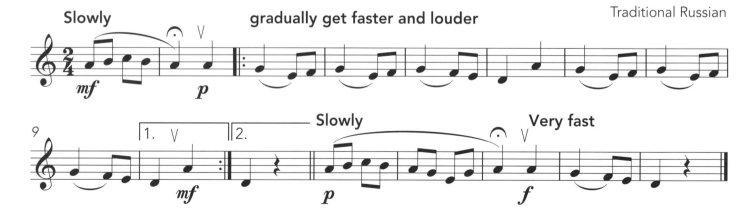

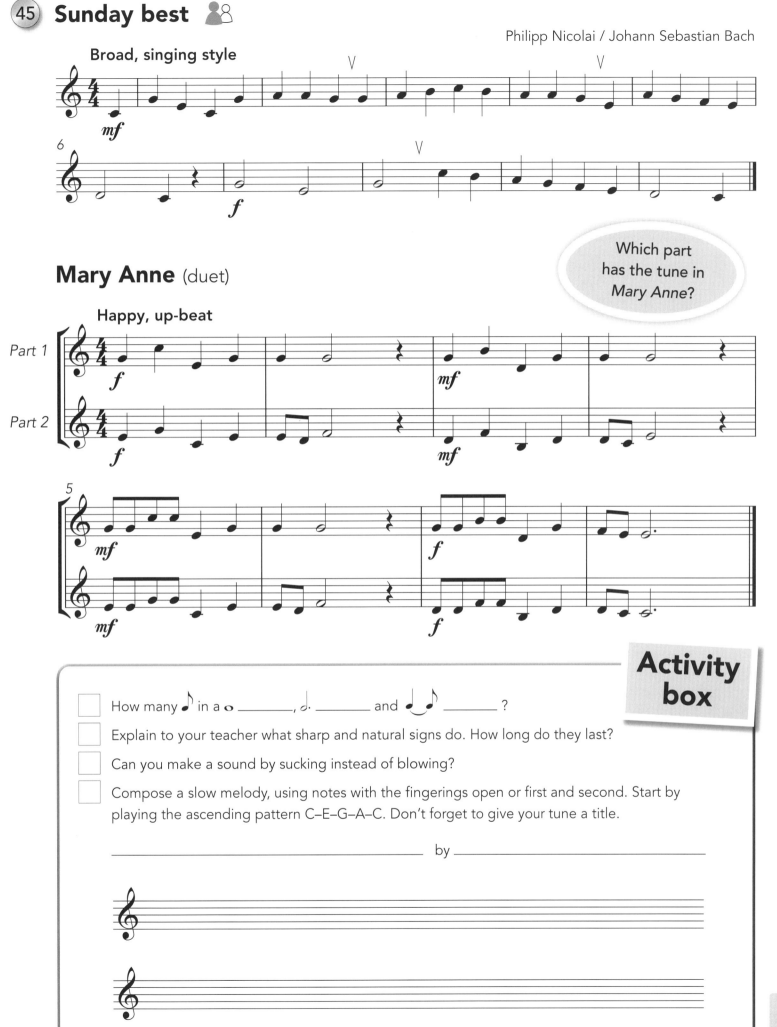

45 **Sunday best**

Philipp Nicolai / Johann Sebastian Bach

Broad, singing style

Mary Anne (duet)

Which part has the tune in *Mary Anne*?

Happy, up-beat

Part 1

Part 2

Activity box

How many ♪ in a 𝅝 _____, 𝅗𝅥. _____ and ♩♪ _____ ?

Explain to your teacher what sharp and natural signs do. How long do they last?

Can you make a sound by sucking instead of blowing?

Compose a slow melody, using notes with the fingerings open or first and second. Start by playing the ascending pattern C–E–G–A–C. Don't forget to give your tune a title.

_____ by _____

27

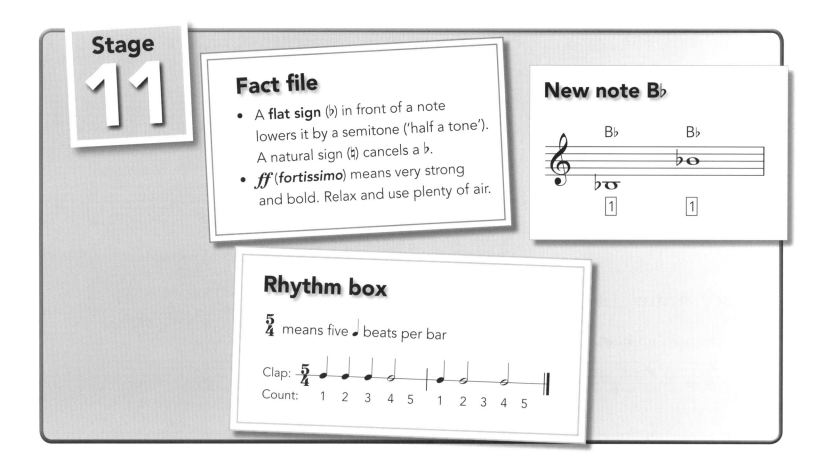

Fact file

- A **flat sign** (♭) in front of a note lowers it by a semitone ('half a tone'). A natural sign (♮) cancels a ♭.
- *ff* (**fortissimo**) means very strong and bold. Relax and use plenty of air.

New note B♭

Rhythm box

$\frac{5}{4}$ means five ♩ beats per bar

Clap: ...
Count: 1 2 3 4 5 1 2 3 4 5

Chops exercise

Make an even sound.

46 Yankee Doodle

Traditional American

Cheekily

47 In five 🎹

Long notes

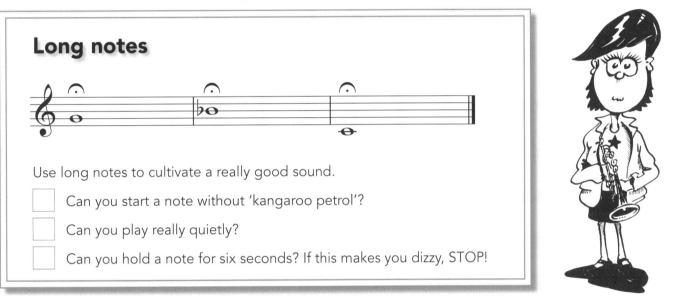

Use long notes to cultivate a really good sound.

☐ Can you start a note without 'kangaroo petrol'?

☐ Can you play really quietly?

☐ Can you hold a note for six seconds? If this makes you dizzy, STOP!

48 Simple gifts (duet) 🎹

Traditional American

Mind the gap! (trio)

Even more lively

Top tips

- A daily 'warm up' gets you ready for good quality playing.
- Mouthpiece buzzing gets everything going.
- Long notes help you make a good sound.
- Lip slurs help your 'chops' (lip muscles) get stronger.
- Scales help your brain, fingers and tongue remember what to do.

☐ Choose your favourite scale and play it upside down!

☐ Give your teacher a lesson on how to play:

1 Loudly

2 Softly

3 Long notes

☐ Write a four-bar rhythm in $\frac{5}{4}$ on the note B♭:

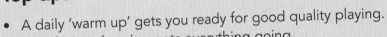

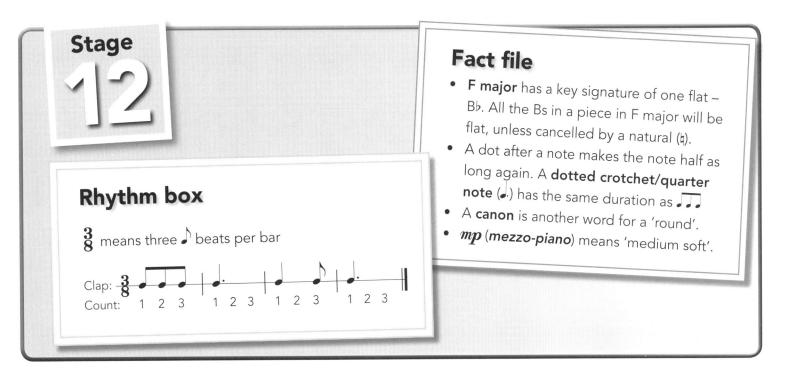

Rhythm box

$\frac{3}{8}$ means three ♪ beats per bar

Clap:
Count: 1 2 3 | 1 2 3 | 1 2 3 | 1 2 3

Fact file

* **F major** has a key signature of one flat – B♭. All the Bs in a piece in F major will be flat, unless cancelled by a natural (♮).
* A dot after a note makes the note half as long again. A **dotted crotchet/quarter note** (♩.) has the same duration as ♪♪♪.
* A **canon** is another word for a 'round'.
* *mp* (**mezzo-piano**) means 'medium soft'.

Simple F major scale

Try this scale with different rhythmic patterns, as in *Fish 'n' chips variation* (p. 24).

Simple F major arpeggio

Study in F

mp

49 ## Jingle bells

James Pierpoint

Clearly

mf

9

f

Tallis' Canon (for up to four players)

Thomas Tallis

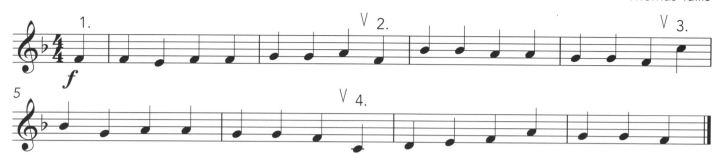

Study in C

Is this familiar? It's useful to be able to play music in more than one key.

Chops' challenge

Pitch game

etc.

Do you know this tune? Can you complete it 'by ear'?

Fingering game

How fast can you play this? Write the note names and fingerings under each note.

Practice

- Play for no more than 15 minutes each day.
- For at least three minutes each day, impress everyone with how quietly you can play.
- Play the difficult bits slowly until they become easy.
- Always play something just for fun.
- Learn your pieces from memory: pop stars never use printed music!

Go down, Moses (trio)

Full note lengths (think TOO—) and quiet control will give this piece real magic.

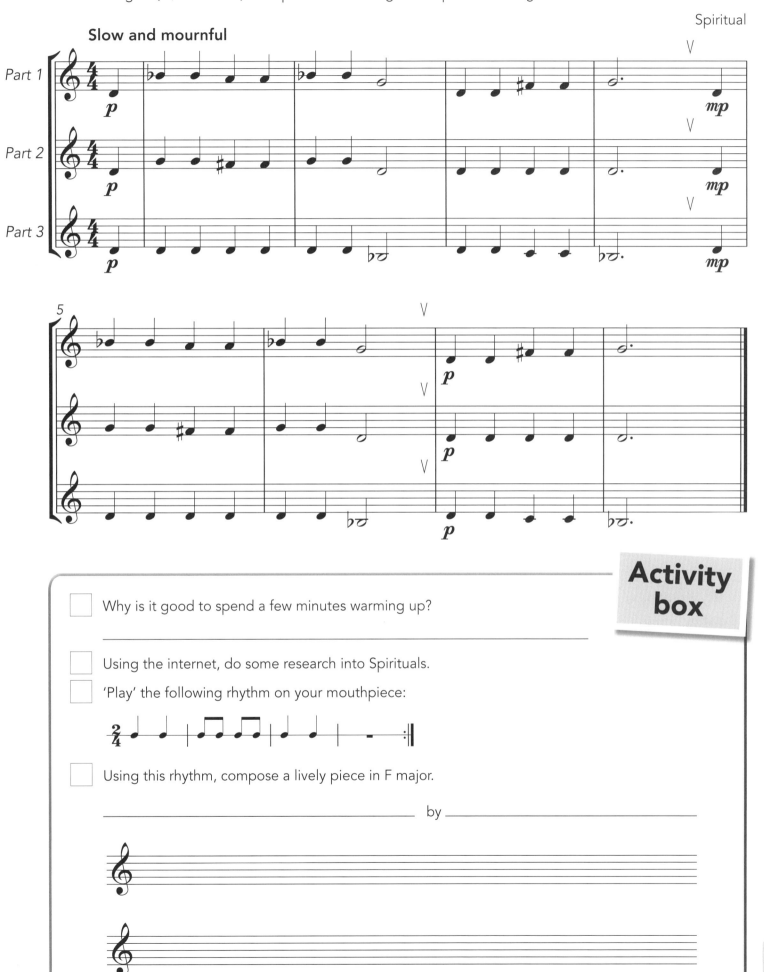

Activity box

☐ Why is it good to spend a few minutes warming up?

_____

☐ Using the internet, do some research into Spirituals.

☐ 'Play' the following rhythm on your mouthpiece:

☐ Using this rhythm, compose a lively piece in F major.

_____ by _____

Concert pieces 1

50 Tuning note: G

Fact file

─**8**─ means rest for 8 bars.

51 Ronde

Tylman Susato

52 Dreaming

Pam Wedgwood

53 Your first hit single

With a good beat

Pam Wedgwood

54 The ballad of the East Neuk

John Miller

Not too slow

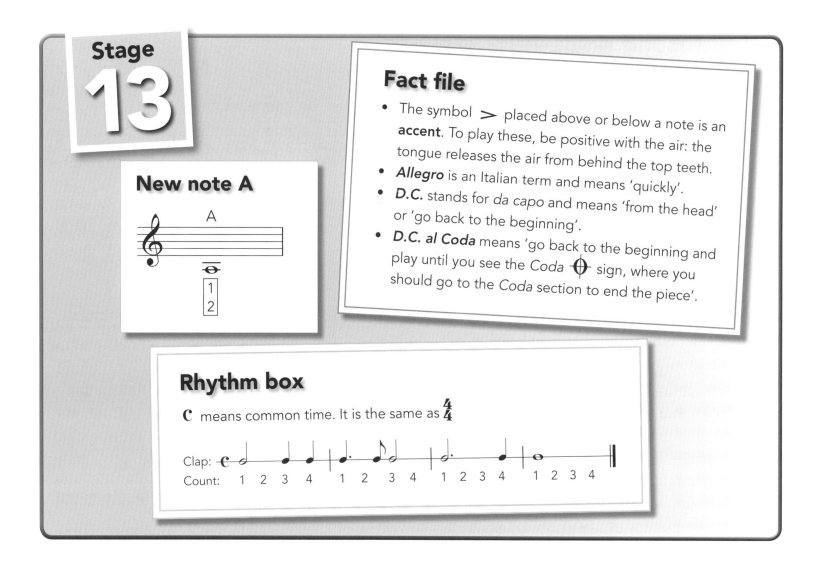

New note A

A

Fact file

- The symbol > placed above or below a note is an **accent**. To play these, be positive with the air: the tongue releases the air from behind the top teeth.
- *Allegro* is an Italian term and means 'quickly'.
- *D.C.* stands for *da capo* and means 'from the head' or 'go back to the beginning'.
- *D.C. al Coda* means 'go back to the beginning and play until you see the *Coda* ⊕ sign, where you should go to the *Coda* section to end the piece'.

Rhythm box

C means common time. It is the same as 4/4

Clap:

Count: 1 2 3 4   1 2 3 4   1 2 3 4   1 2 3 4

Chops exercise

Make a full, even sound.

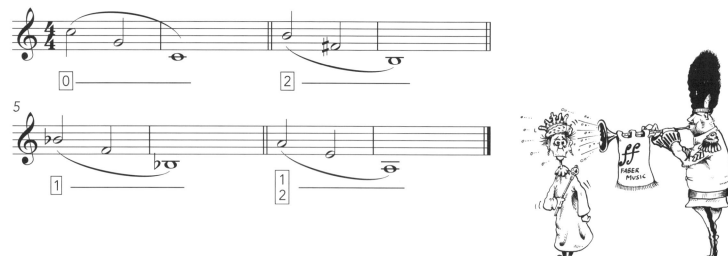

God save the Queen

Mentally subdivide ♩ into 3 ♪ to play this rhythm really well.

Broadly

Anonymous

mf

55 **Sharpen that tongue**

56 *

57 **Aura Lee**

58 **O come, all ye faithful**

59 *

* orchestrated version

Merrily we fanfare (trio)

Traditional

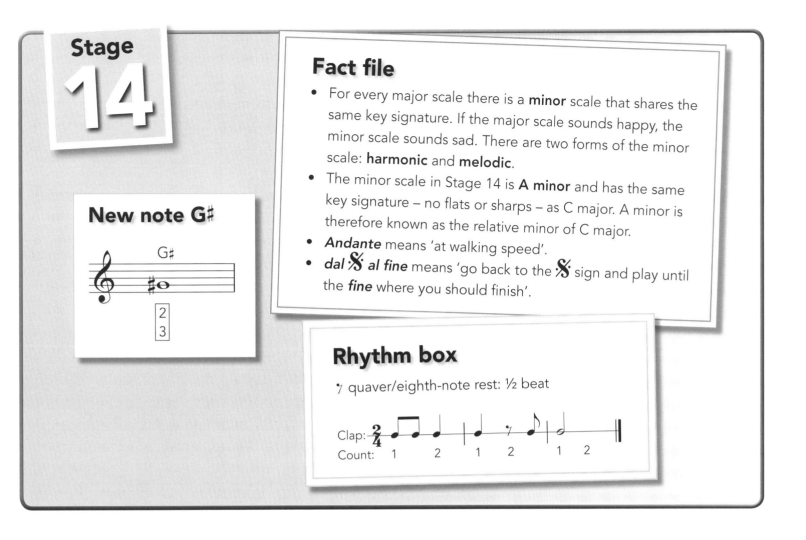

Fact file

- For every major scale there is a **minor** scale that shares the same key signature. If the major scale sounds happy, the minor scale sounds sad. There are two forms of the minor scale: **harmonic** and **melodic**.
- The minor scale in Stage 14 is **A minor** and has the same key signature – no flats or sharps – as C major. A minor is therefore known as the relative minor of C major.
- **Andante** means 'at walking speed'.
- **dal 𝄋 al fine** means 'go back to the 𝄋 sign and play until the **fine** where you should finish'.

New note G♯

Rhythm box

♩ quaver/eighth-note rest: ½ beat

Low notes – A minor (harmonic)

Challenge

Try this back to front and in different rhythms too – it's great for improving your low notes.

A minor scale (melodic)

Play this scale in as many different ways as possible – see Stage 9 for some ideas.

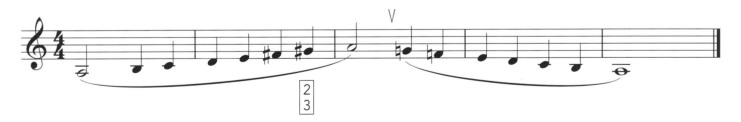

A minor arpeggios

60 Winter

Traditional Polish

Andante

61 The happy ending

Brisk and lifted

La follia (duet)

Arcangelo Corelli

Slow and stately

Nina Rota

Top tip

When you breathe in, always relax: think of a half-yawn.

Top tip

Low notes need an open throat and plenty of air. Thinking of the words TAW— or BAH— can help.

Activity box

☐ Clap this rhythm:

☐ What's the relative major of A minor? _____

☐ What's your *embouchure*? You may have to ask your teacher this one!

_____

☐ Try playing *Happy Birthday* and *Amazing Grace* by ear (from memory) – start on a C. (Both are in the key of F major.)

☐ Try writing a sad piece in the key of A minor. Remember to give it a title.

_____ by _____

New note D

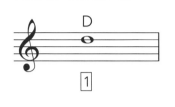

Fact file

- The symbol ◁══ or the word **crescendo** means 'get louder'.
- The symbol ══▷ or the word **diminuendo** means 'get quieter'.
- A line above or below a note ͞ is called **tenuto** and means 'lean on the note'.
- A dot ˙ is called **staccato** and means 'short and detached'.
- **Rit.** (**Ritardando**) means 'gradually getting slower'. (**A tempo** means 'back to the original speed'.)

Rhythm box

¢ means 'cut time': feel two ♩ beats per bar

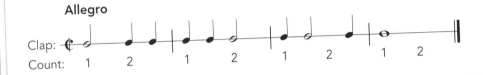

Allegro

Clap:
Count: 1 2 1 2 1 2 1 2

Top tip

Flow the air faster for the higher notes.

Airflow exercise

(63) ## Loch Lomond 🎹

Traditional Scottish

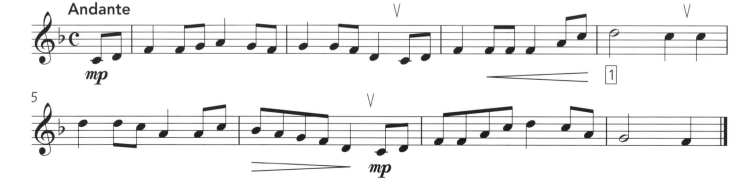

64 Scarborough Fair 🎹

Traditional English

Frère Jacques (round)

You can play *Frère Jacques* as a round with up to 4 players.

Traditional French

65 For His Majesty's Sagbutts and Cornetts 🎹
66*

Can you spot the hidden melody?

* orchestrated version

⑥⑦ Simple G major scale 🎹

⑥⑦ Simple G major arpeggio 🎹

Top tip

To play high notes think of the syllable TEE— and use firm tummy muscles.

Mack the Knife ('Moritat') from *The Threepenny Opera* (trio)

Play this together in a smooth, smoochy version and then in a loud brash style.

Kurt Weill

Stage 16

New note C#

Fact file

- **D major** has a key signature of two sharps – F# and C#.
- Some pieces are written in **mixed meter**. This means that the pulse continues throughout, but the time signature changes.
- An **off beat** is a note that goes against the beat. Another name for this is a 'syncopated note'.
- When playing a low C# (or D♭), push out the third slide extension by about 2cm. This note is usually very sharp.
- When playing a low D, push out the same slide, but less far.

D major scale and arpeggio

Practise this in different ways (tongued, slurred and from memory).

68 ## Can-can

Jacques Offenbach

69 ## Country dance

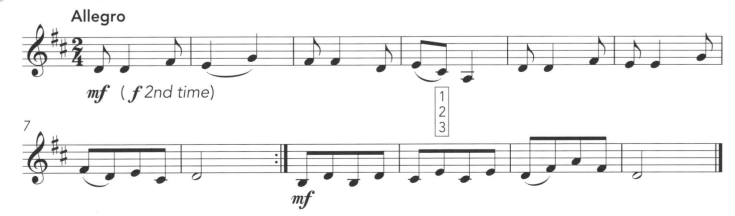

70 Promenade 🎹

This piece is in mixed meter. Keep the ♩ pulse steady throughout.

Modest Mussorgsky

71 The first Nowell 🎹

Traditional English carol

> A 4/4 bar can be divided up in lots of ways but … Don't panic!

Don't panic (duet)

72 Cornish dance

Malcolm Arnold

Top tip

Look after your teeth.
You will need them to
play well.

Activity box

☐ Clap this rhythm:

Allegro

☐ What can help to play high notes well? _____

☐ What's an ear trumpet? _____

☐ Using first valve only, you now have a choice of four notes you can play.
Write the note names here.

_____

☐ Experiment with these notes, and compose two fanfares for your school sports day:
one fast and exciting, one slow and impressive.

1.

2.

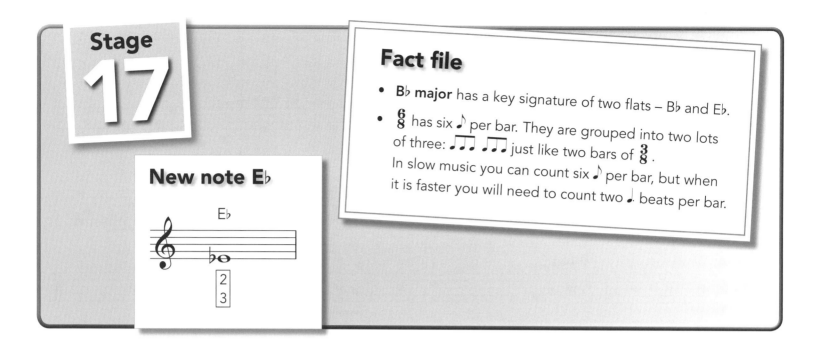

Stage 17

New note E♭

Fact file

- **B♭ major** has a key signature of two flats – B♭ and E♭.
- $\frac{6}{8}$ has six ♪ per bar. They are grouped into two lots of three: ♫♪ ♫♪ just like two bars of $\frac{3}{8}$.
  In slow music you can count six ♪ per bar, but when it is faster you will need to count two ♩. beats per bar.

Chops exercise

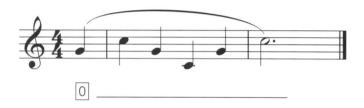

Top tip

Make an even, open sound. Always relax when you breathe in: think of a half-yawn.

Repeat the pattern with these fingerings:

B♭ major scale

B♭ major arpeggios

48

Joy to the world

after George Frideric Handel

Joyful, heraldic

* orchestrated version

Frankie and Johnny

Traditional blues

Steady stomp

Drink to me only

Slowly

Traditional

Row your boat (round)

Allegro

Traditional

Here we go round the mulberry bush (trio)

Traditional

Rhythmic and jolly

Top tip

Gradually increase the speed until you can feel this tune as 2-in-the-bar.

TICK-TOCK...

True or false?

| ? | The dots above or below a note are called *legato*. _____ |

| ? | B♭ major has a key signature of two flats. _____ |

| ? | *Rit*. means gradually getting slower. _____ |

| ? | **6/8** has three ♩. beats per bar. _____ |

| ? | ¢ means two ♩ beats per bar. _____ |

50

Stage
18

Top tip

When playing chromatic passages, the way you hold the instrument really matters. Keep your right-hand fingers slightly bent, and always on the valve caps.

Fact file

- A **chromatic scale** moves up or down in semitone steps, or *chromatically*, using all twelve pitches. *Chroma* is a Greek word meaning 'colour'.
- The same note can often have more than one name, depending on context, e.g. A♭ is the same pitch as G♯; these are called **enharmonic** notes.
- *Espressivo* is the Italian word for 'expressive'.

Chromatic scale

Nimble fingers

76 · ## French march

Jean-Baptiste Arban

51

77 'O sole mio

Eduardo di Capua

Andante espressivo

Batman (trio)

Neil Hefti

Steady, very rhythmic

Part 1

Part 2

Part 3

BAT- MAN! (play or shout)

Marche slave (trio)

Play this with a full, well-sustained sound.

Pyotr Ilyich Tchaikovsky

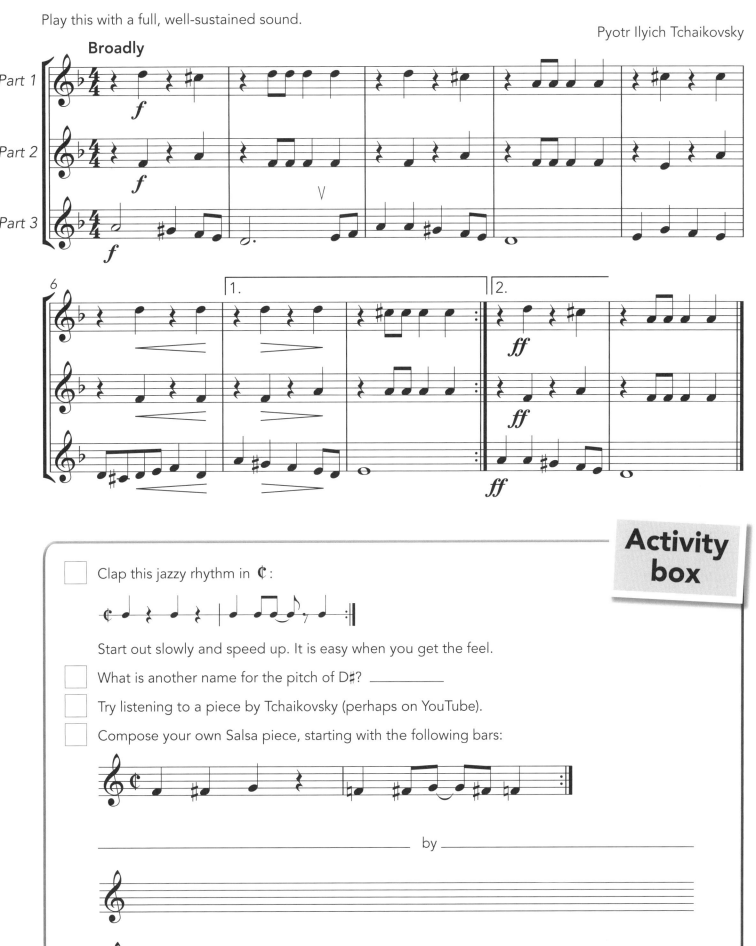

Activity box

☐ Clap this jazzy rhythm in ¢:

Start out slowly and speed up. It is easy when you get the feel.

☐ What is another name for the pitch of D♯? _____

☐ Try listening to a piece by Tchaikovsky (perhaps on YouTube).

☐ Compose your own Salsa piece, starting with the following bars:

_____ by _____

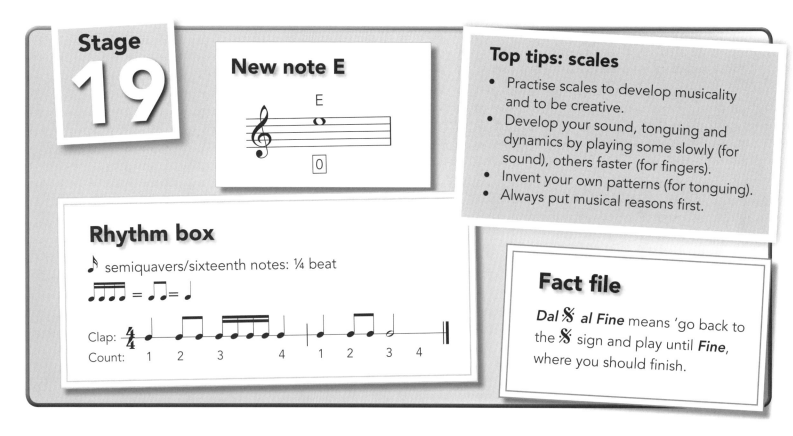

New note E

Top tips: scales
- Practise scales to develop musicality and to be creative.
- Develop your sound, tonguing and dynamics by playing some slowly (for sound), others faster (for fingers).
- Invent your own patterns (for tonguing).
- Always put musical reasons first.

Rhythm box

♪ semiquavers/sixteenth notes: ¼ beat

Fact file

Dal 𝄋 al Fine means 'go back to the 𝄋 sign and play until *Fine*, where you should finish.

D minor scale (harmonic)

D minor scale (melodic)

D minor arpeggio

Airflow exercise

Use these phrases to extend your range. Try them played normally and buzzed on the mouthpiece.
Don't force – the top notes will come.

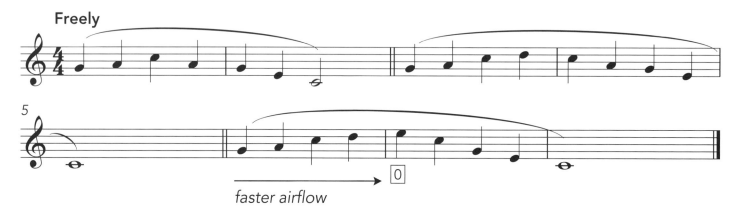

faster airflow

54

Know your tunes!

Fill in the name and the key of each tune – and then finish each one by ear!

1

Tune: _____

Key: _____

2

Tune: _____

Key: _____

3

Tune: _____

Key: _____

Have a Coke Cola

Neatly

Have a Co - ke Co - la

William Tell

Gioachino Rossini

Allegro

mp

Fine

mf

dal 𝄋 al Fine

mp

* orchestrated version

55

Nice one, Johann (duet)

Johann Sebastian Bach

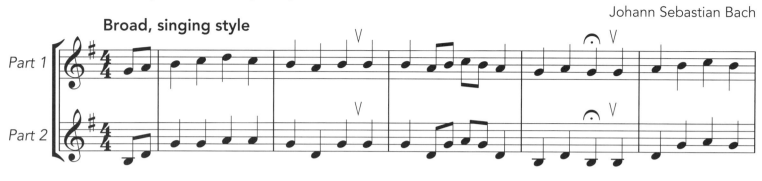

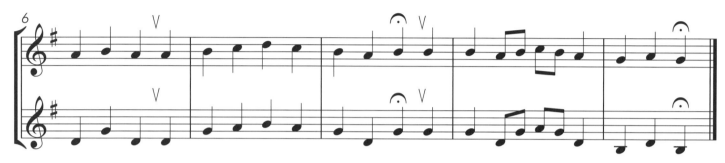

80 ## Blue-note blues

Top tip

Always try to break your playing up into 15-minute sessions. Keep your lips and brain fresh.

Activity box

- How many different pitches are there in the chromatic scale? _____
- What can you remember about posture and breathing? Do these things help you play with ease?
- If brass instruments are made of brass, and woodwind instruments are made of wood, what are string instruments made of? _____
- Invent your own tonguing exercise, using the rhythm ♩♫♩ or ♩♫

Stage 20

Chromatic warm-up

Always limber up your chops and fingers so you can improvise well.

play 3 times

Blues scale of D

Top tip

Experiment with your own versions of scales; play them with:
- different rhythms
- different dynamics
- different articulation
- at different speeds.

Try to match them to style of the piece you are about to play.

Funky blues scale

Rock improvisation (duet)

Note bank   **Ideas bank**

Player 1

Player 2

* orchestrated version

Player 2
Start on your own.
Keep a solid pulse throughout.

Player 1
Wait a few bars before joining in, then improvise using the notes in your note bank. There are four idea banks to get you going – start with these and then make up your own.

Rock march

Try improvising the second time through.

Free improvisation (3 or more players)

This is completely different from the previous rock improvisation, with no steady beat throughout.

- Choose your own notes from the note bank. All are either open or first valve.
- As a group, create your own moods and images.
- Decide group patterns, textures and volume.
- Experiment with the ideas given below, then invent your own.
- Remember, in a group it is important to listen as well as play.

And don't forget a title … how about **London Eye**, or **Dracula**?

Note bank

Ideas bank

melodic

powerful

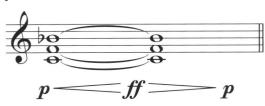

rhythmic

mysterious

Concert pieces 2

84 Tuning note: High C

85 ## Lancaster Lullaby 🎹

Moderato

John Miller

86 ## Flashback 🎹

Disco style, lively

Pam Wedgwood

87 Twelfth Street Rag

Euday L Bowman

The wild man

(88) (spoken introduction) (89) (fast) (90) (very fast)

(91) Sweeny Todd

Malcolm Arnold

Congratulations!

Well done for finishing this book and good luck with your future playing!

Fingering chart

The cornet and trumpet are both similar to a bugle.
Each plays an identical pattern of notes when no valves are pressed down.
Putting down one or more valves lengthens the tube and changes the pitch
of the pattern.

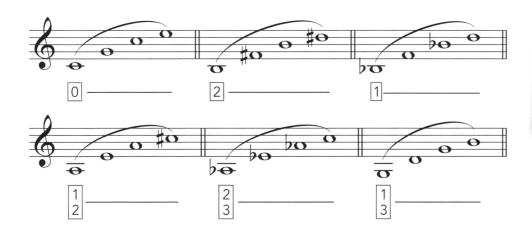

Top tip

Also try this with all three valves down.

When the patterns above are linked together, you can play all the chromatic notes:

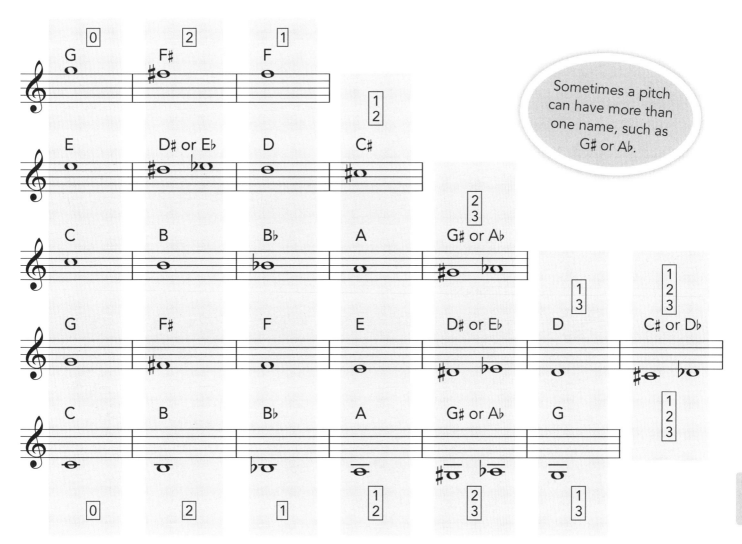

Sometimes a pitch can have more than one name, such as G♯ or A♭.

Acknowledgements

Many colleagues and students have helped me write this book. However, composer Pam Wedgwood, illustrator Drew Hillier, and a lively and expert editorial team at Faber Music have been major contributors, ever helpful and creative at all stages.

Additional resources

The Basics series
Trumpet Basics: Teacher's book
The Basics website (**www.fabermusicstore.com/basics**) contains further resources including in-depth teaching notes to use in conjunction with *Trumpet Basics*.

Also available from Faber Music
Graded Exercises and Studies for Trumpet
Team Brass

New edition © 2013 by Faber Music Ltd
First published in 2002 by Faber Music Ltd
Bloomsbury House
74–77 Great Russell Street
London WC1B 3DA
Music processed by Jeanne Roberts
Cover design by Chloë Alexander
Design by Susan Clarke
Photographs, page 4: Yamaha-Kemble Music (UK) Ltd
Printed in England by Caligraving Ltd
All rights reserved

ISBN10: 0-571-51998-9 / 0-571-52286-6
EAN13: 978-0-571-51998-9 / 978-0-571-52286-6

To buy Faber Music publications or to find out about the full range of titles available please contact your local music retailer or Faber Music sales enquiries:

Faber Music Ltd, Burnt Mill, Elizabeth Way, Harlow CM20 2HX England
Tel: +44 (0)1279 82 89 82   Fax: +44 (0)1279 82 89 83
sales@fabermusic.com   fabermusic.com